HAPPY BIRTHDAY
FELIZ CUMPLEAÑOS

A Traditional Song in English, Spanish, and American Sign Language

By NICHOLAS IAN

Illustrated by LUKE SÉGUIN MAGEE

Music Arranged and Produced by STEVEN C MUSIC

CANTATA
LEARNING

WWW.CANTATALEARNING.COM

CANTATA LEARNING

Published by Cantata Learning
1710 Roe Crest Drive
North Mankato, MN 56003
www.cantatalearning.com

Library of Congress Control Number: 2015958645
Ian, Nicholas
    Happy Birthday / Feliz Cumpleaños : A Traditional Song in English, Spanish, and
American Sign Language / by Nicholas Ian; Illustrated by Luke Séguin Magee
    Series: Sing-along Songs
    Audience: Ages: 3–9; Grades: PreK–4
    Summary: A classic birthday song sung in English, Spanish, and American Sign Language.
    ISBN: 978-1-63290-760-8 (library binding/CD)
    ISBN: 978-1-63290-761-5 (paperback/CD)
    1. Stories in rhyme. 2. Birthday celebrations—nonfiction.

Book design and art direction, Tim Palin Creative
Editorial direction, Flat Sole Studio
Music direction, Elizabeth Draper
Music arranged and produced by Steven C Music
American Sign Language consultant, Paddy Shelden
Spanish Language Consultant, Leah Mark, Minnesota Licensed K-12 Spanish Teacher

Printed in the United States of America in North Mankato, Minnesota.
102016   0352CGS16R

ACCESS THE MUSIC!

SCAN
CODE
WITH
MOBILE
APP

CANTATALEARNING.COM

A birthday celebrates when a person was born.
All over the world, people celebrate birthdays in
different ways. Some people celebrate with friends
and family by singing a special song. "Happy
Birthday" is sung all around the world.

In this story, a class sings in English, Spanish, and American Sign Language. Turn the page and sing along with them!

Happy birthday to you,
Happy birthday to you,
Happy birthday dear friend,
Happy birthday to you!

Feliz cumpleaños a ti,

Feliz cumpleaños a ti,

Feliz cumpleaños querido amigo,

Feliz cumpleaños a ti!

Happy birthday to you,
Happy birthday to you,
Happy birthday dear friend,
Happy birthday to you!

Feliz cumpleaños a ti,

Feliz cumpleaños a ti,

Feliz cumpleaños querido amigo,

Feliz cumpleaños a ti!

Happy birthday to you,
Happy birthday to you,
Happy birthday dear friend,
Happy birthday to you!

Feliz cumpleaños a ti,

Feliz cumpleaños a ti,

Feliz cumpleaños querido amigo,

Feliz cumpleaños a ti!

Happy birthday to you,
Happy birthday to you,
Happy birthday dear friend,
Happy birthday to you!

Feliz cumpleaños a ti,

Feliz cumpleaños a ti,

Feliz cumpleaños querido amigo,

Feliz cumpleaños a ti!

SONG LYRICS
Happy Birthday

Happy birthday to you,
Happy birthday to you,
Happy birthday dear friend,
Happy birthday to you!

Feliz cumpleaños a ti,
Feliz cumpleaños a ti,
Feliz cumpleaños querido amigo,
Feliz cumpleaños a ti!

Happy birthday to you,
Happy birthday to you,
Happy birthday dear friend,
Happy birthday to you!

Feliz cumpleaños a ti,
Feliz cumpleaños a ti,
Feliz cumpleaños querido amigo,
Feliz cumpleaños a ti!

Happy birthday to you,
Happy birthday to you,
Happy birthday dear friend,
Happy birthday to you!

Feliz cumpleaños a ti,
Feliz cumpleaños a ti,
Feliz cumpleaños querido amigo,
Feliz cumpleaños a ti!

Happy birthday to you,
Happy birthday to you,
Happy birthday dear friend,
Happy birthday to you!

Feliz cumpleaños a ti,
Feliz cumpleaños a ti,
Feliz cumpleaños querido amigo,
Feliz cumpleaños a ti!

Happy Birthday

New Orleans Brass Band
Steven C Music

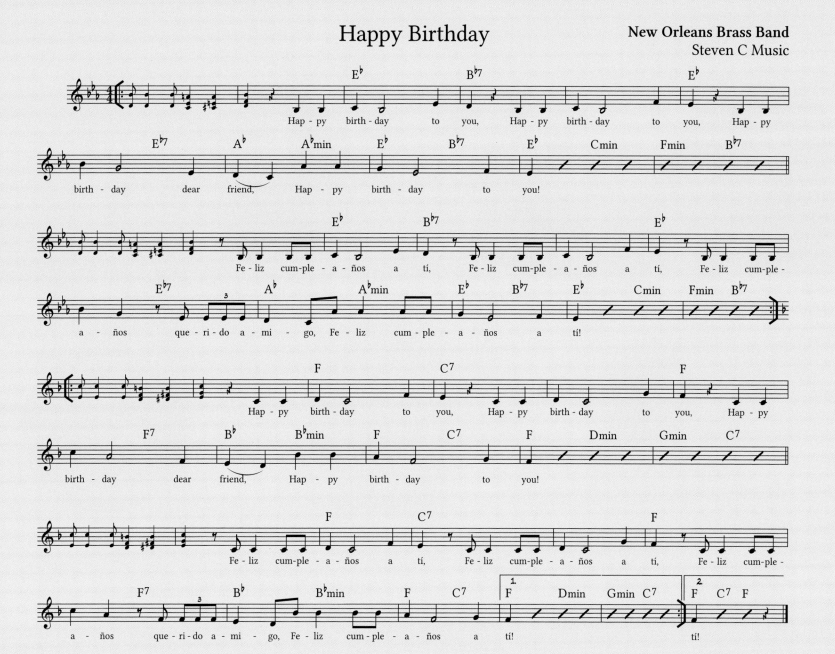

Hap - py birth - day to you, Hap - py birth - day to you, Hap - py birth - day dear friend, Hap - py birth - day to you!

Fe - liz cum-ple - a - ños a tí, Fe - liz cum-ple - a - ños a tí, Fe - liz cum-ple - a - ños que - ri - do a - mi - go, Fe - liz cum-ple - a - ños a tí!

Hap - py birth - day to you, Hap - py birth - day to you, Hap - py birth - day dear friend, Hap - py birth - day to you!

Fe - liz cum-ple - a - ños a tí, Fe - liz cum-ple - a - ños a tí, Fe - liz cum-ple - a - ños que - ri - do a - mi - go, Fe - liz cum-ple - a - ños a tí! tí!

23

GLOSSARY

happy

birthday

to

you

dear (love, dearly loved)

friend

TO LEARN MORE

Clay, Kathryn. *Signing at School: Sign Language for Kids*. North Mankato, MN: Capstone Press, 2014.

Jules, Jacqueline. *Abuela's Birthday*. North Mankato, MN: Picture Window Books, 2015.

Numeroff, Laura. *Happy Birthday, Mouse!* New York: Balzer & Bray, 2012.

Yolen, Jane, and Mark Teague. *How Do Dinosaurs Say Happy Birthday?* New York: Blue Sky Press, 2011.